Watch It Grow

Watch a Bean Grow

by Kirsten Chang

Bullfrog Books

Ideas for Parents and Teachers

Bullfrog Books let children practice reading informational text at the earliest reading levels. Repetition, familiar words, and photo labels support early readers.

Before Reading

- Discuss the cover photo. What does it tell them?

- Look at the picture glossary together. Read and discuss the words.

Read the Book

- "Walk" through the book and look at the photos. Let the child ask questions. Point out the photo labels.

- Read the book to the child, or have him or her read independently.

After Reading

- Prompt the child to think more. Ask: Do you like to eat beans? Can you explain how they grow?

Bullfrog Books are published by Jump!
5357 Penn Avenue South
Minneapolis, MN 55419
www.jumplibrary.com

Library of Congress Cataloging-in-Publication Data

Names: Chang, Kirsten, author.
Title: Watch a bean grow / by Kirsten Chang.
Description: Bullfrog books edition.
Minneapolis, MN: Jump!, Inc., [2019]
Series: Watch it grow | Audience: Age 5–8.
Audience: K to Grade 3. | Includes index.
Identifiers: LCCN 2018017782 (print)
LCCN 2018018322 (ebook)
ISBN 9781641282574 (ebook)
ISBN 9781641282550 (hardcover: alk. paper)
ISBN 9781641282567 (paperback)
Subjects: LCSH: Beans—Juvenile literature.
Beans—Life cycles—Juvenile literature.
Classification: LCC SB327 (ebook)
LCC SB327 .C43 2019 (print) | DDC 633.3—dc23
LC record available at https://lccn.loc.gov/2018017782

Editor: Jenna Trnka
Designer: Michelle Sonnek

Photo Credits: Sandra Caldwell/Shutterstock, cover; feellife/iStock, 1; Shutterstock, 3; Daisy-Daisy/iStock, 4; Fotokostic/Shutterstock, 5; Galayko Sergey/Shutterstock, 6–7; Billion Photos/Shutterstock, 8–9; redmal/iStock, 10–11 (plant), 22mr, 23tr, 23bl; Andrey_Kuzmin/Shutterstock, 10–11 (soil), 23bl; Zeljko Radojko/Shutterstock, 12–13; Potapov Alexander/Shutterstock, 14, 22br; giedre vaitekune/Shutterstock, 15, 22bl, 23tm; tab62/Shutterstock, 16–17, 22ml, 23br; oksana2010/Shutterstock, 18; Tawin Mukdharakosa/Shutterstock, 19, 23tl; Jose Luis Pelaez Inc/Getty, 20–21; Siaivo/Shutterstock, 22t; WitthayaP/Shutterstock, 24.

Printed in the United States of America at Corporate Graphics in North Mankato, Minnesota.

Table of Contents

Mia picks beans.

How do
beans grow?

There are many
kinds of beans.

They grow
from seeds.

A bean is a seed.

A farmer plants
seeds in the soil.

It is spring.

It must be warm
for beans to grow.

bean
seed

stem

root

The seed gets water.

It opens.

A root grows down.

A stem grows up.

The stem grows leaves.

The leaves get sun.

leaf

Flowers grow.

flower

pod

Then pods grow.
The pods have
beans inside!

Different beans
are picked at
different times.

Green beans
are picked when
they are tender.

Dry beans are left on the plant until they are hard.

Some are canned.

Tim likes green beans. Yum!

Life Cycle of a Bean

How does a green bean grow?

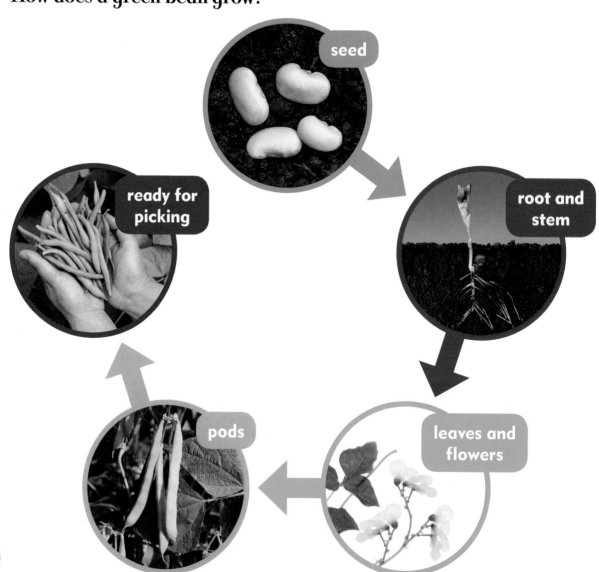

seed

root and stem

leaves and flowers

pods

ready for picking

Picture Glossary

canned
Placed and
preserved in
a sealed can.

pods
Long, thin cases
that grow on
some plants and
contain seeds.

root
Part of a plant that
grows underground
and gets water and
food from the soil.

soil
Another word
for dirt.

stem
The long, thin
part of a plant
that grows leaves
and flowers.

tender
Soft and easy
to eat.

Index

To Learn More

Learning more is as easy as 1, 2, 3.

1) Go to www.factsurfer.com

2) Enter "watchabeangrow" into the search box.

3) Click the "Surf" button to see a list of websites.

With factsurfer.com, finding more information is just a click away.